Score

My Trio Book

The Music of
Suzuki Violin School, Volumes 1 and 2
arranged for three violins

by Kerstin Wartberg

Mein Trio-Buch

Die Musikstücke der Suzuki-Violinschule
Heft 1 und 2
arrangiert für drei Geigen

Sole publisher for the entire world except Japan:
Summy-Birchard Inc.
exclusively distributed by
Warner Bros. Publications
15800 N.W. 48th Avenue, Miami, Florida 33014

ISBN 1-58951-196-4

Foreword

How wondrous is the life-force! One feels it everywhere. Through it we can enjoy the beauty of nature. Tiny buds become magical flowers, every morning the birds begin to sing, and countless leaves, grasses, and flowers herald to us the great life-force. In addition to the magnificence of nature, we have also been given the gift of music. Music is the language of the spirit and should purify us and open our hearts for the sublime. We need to recognize that this gift is to be used. Sixty years ago, when I recognized the scope and mighty power of nature's developmental principles and realized that every child in the world learns his mother tongue without difficulty, I changed the outlook on my life and made countless discoveries. We should all learn to be an integral part of creation and not to oppose the life-force. Once this is learned, we can reach unbelievable heights.

Our task as parents and teachers is to raise our children to be worthy people who will be able to assume responsibility for the further development of the world. Much is to be done. With courage, enterprise, and gratitude for the life-force that is given to us, we can travel this road together.

Kerstin Wartberg was the first German to study at and graduate from the Talent Education Institute in Matsumoto, Japan. In the many years since then, my wife and I have been in close contact with her. I am pleased that she wants to share my teaching method and philosophy with the interested reader. I wish her publication a large circulation and hope that it falls on fertile ground.

Matsumoto, June 1994

Dr. Shinichi Suzuki

Vorwort

Wie wundervoll wirkt die Lebenskraft! Überall ist sie zu spüren. Sie ermöglicht, daß wir uns an der Schönheit der Natur erfreuen können. Wir beobachten, wie die Knospen sich zu zauberhaften Blüten öffnen, wie jeden Morgen die Vögel wieder zu singen beginnen und wie unzählige Blätter, Gräser und Blumen uns von der großen Lebenskraft künden wollen. Zu der herrlichen Natur ist uns außerdem noch die Musik geschenkt worden. Musik ist die Sprache des Geistes und soll uns läutern und für Höheres öffnen. Wir Menschen müssen erkennen, daß wir diese Geschenke nutzen sollen. Als ich vor etwa 60 Jahren den Umfang und die gewaltige Kraft der natürlichen Entwicklungsgesetze erkannte und feststellte, wie jedes Kind auf der Welt seine Muttersprache problemlos erlernt, habe ich mein Leben umgestellt und danach unzählige Entdeckungen gemacht. Wir alle sollten lernen, uns nicht gegen die Lebenskraft zu stellen, sondern uns in die Schöpfung einzufügen. Dann werden wir, von den großen Hilfen gestärkt, unglaubliche Höhen erreichen können.

Die Aufgabe der Eltern und Lehrer ist, unsere Kinder zu wertvollen Menschen zu erziehen, die später einmal die Verantwortung für die Weiterentwicklung der Welt übernehmen können. Vieles ist zu tun. Mit Mut, Tatkraft und Dankbarkeit für die uns geschenkte Lebenskraft können wir den Weg gemeinsam gehen.

Kerstin Wartberg war die erste Deutsche, die am Talent Education Institute in Matsumoto/Japan studierte und graduierte. Sie steht seitdem nun schon über viele Jahre mit meiner Frau und mir in enger Verbindung. Ich freue mich, daß sie meine Unterrichtsweise aus methodisch-didaktischer und aus übergeordneter Sicht dem interessierten Leser nahebringen will. So wünsche ich ihren Veröffentlichungen eine weite Verbreitung und hoffe, daß sie auf fruchtbaren Boden fallen werden.

Matsumoto, Juni 1994

Dr. Shinichi Suzuki

Contents - Inhaltsverzeichnis

I. Volume 1 - Heft 1

II. Volume 2 - Heft 2

Introduction

This book contains all of the pieces from Volumes 1 and 2 of the Suzuki Violin School arranged for three violins. They can be played with or without piano accompaniment, which expands their performance possibilities. A performance in the park, in kindergarten, or in the yard of the music school can now take place even without the help of a piano.

***My Trio Book*: a new possibility for ensembles of students with very different levels of ability.**
Another advantage of these arrangements is that students with different levels of playing and reading ability can make music together. On the next page is a table listing the grade of difficulty for each piece and each part. The teacher can, for example, easily pick out pieces that can be played together by a beginner in Volume 1, a beginning reader, and an advanced student.

***My Trio Book*: a reading course for the beginning reader.** Learning the individual parts stepwise is equivalent to the systematic method used to teach note reading. Detailed instructions can be found in the section "Dear Children" on page 8.

A table listing the reading demands of each piece is found on the last pages of the separate booklets for the second and third violin parts. This table should be studied closely before working on a piece. The student can see at a glance what is required to read the piece, and any specific deficiencies can be improved.

***My Trio Book* provides an entirely new musical inspiration via the CD.** It includes the trio arrangements of all the pieces from Volumes 1 and 2. The tempi are purposely somewhat slower than on other recordings of the Suzuki literature. This enables students to read along more easily and feel their way into the three-part ensemble playing. To indicate tempo and character, each piece begins with a short harp introduction. Hearing and playing familiar pieces in new arrangements will musically inspire the student and awaken a sense for nuance and finesse. The CD is meant for students to listen to as well as to play along with.

***My Trio Book*: an elementary school of ensemble playing.** All the parts were purposely kept as simple as possible, not for compositional elegance but rather for ease of playing music in three parts. After the notes have been learned, the real work can begin: improving the quality of the ensemble playing. The main teaching focus should be the adjustments among the various voices with regard to intonation, rhythm, dynamics, articulation, phrasing, bowing, breathing together, beginning and ending phrases together, and so on. Thorough work along these lines will be rewarded with a full ensemble sound and a solid ability to play together, giving joy not only to those making the music but also to the kind listeners.

Kerstin Wartberg

Einführung

Im vorliegenden Band befinden sich alle Stücke der Suzuki-Violinschule von Heft 1 und 2, arrangiert für drei Geigen. Diese können sowohl mit als auch ohne Klavier gespielt werden, wodurch die Bandbreite der Vorspielmöglichkeiten sinnvoll erweitert wird. Ein Auftritt im Stadtpark, im Kindergarten oder im Innenhof der Musikschule läßt sich nun auch ohne Zuhilfenahme eines Klaviers problemlos durchführen.

***Mein Trio-Buch* - eine neue Möglichkeit zum Zusammenspiel für Schüler mit stark voneinander abweichenden Fähigkeiten**
Ein weiterer Vorteil besteht darin, Schüler mit ganz unterschiedlichem Spiel- und Notenleseniveau zusammen musizieren zu lassen. Auf der nächsten Seite befindet sich eine Tabelle. Hier sind die Schwierigkeitsstufen jedes Stückes und jeder Stimme übersichtlich dargestellt. Der Lehrer kann somit speziell für den Leistungsstand seiner Schüler geeignete Musikstücke aussuchen und problemlos erkennen, welche Stücke z.B. von einem kleinen Anfänger aus Heft 1, einem Notenleseanfänger und einem fortgeschritteneren Schüler leicht gemeinsam gemeistert werden können.

***Mein Trio-Buch* - ein Notenleselehrgang für die Unterstufe**
Das stufenweise Erlernen der einzelnen Stimmen kommt dem systematischen Notenlese- und Blattspieltraining gleich. Nähere Anleitungen hierzu stehen in dem Abschnitt „Liebe Kinder".

Eine Aufstellung der Notenleseanforderungen für jedes Stück befindet sich auf den letzten Seiten des Einzelheftes der zweiten sowie der dritten Stimme. Vor der Erarbeitung eines neuen Stückes sollte diese Aufstellung genau angeschaut werden. Nun kann der Schüler die konkreten Leseanforderungen leicht überblicken und lückenhafte Kenntnisse gezielt verbessern.

***Mein Trio-Buch* enthält eine ganz neue musikalische Anregung durch die zugehörige CD** Auf der CD sind alle Stücke von Heft 1 und 2 in Trio-Besetzung eingespielt. Die Tempi der Stücke sind absichtlich etwas ruhiger gehalten im Vergleich zu den bisherigen Einspielungen der Suzuki-Stücke. Der Schüler kann sich so beim Notenlesen etwas mehr Zeit nehmen und sich besser in das mehrstimmige Spielen einfühlen.
Um das jeweilige Tempo und den musikalischen Charakter gut zu erfassen, beginnt jedes Stück mit einer kurzen Einleitung, die von einer Harfe gespielt wird. Das Hören und das eigene Musizieren von vertrauten Stücken mit neuen Klangeindrücken wird dem Schüler gewiß viele musikalische Anregungen geben und in ihm einen Sinn für Feinheiten und Nuancen wecken. Die CD ist sowohl zum Anhören als auch zum Mitspielen gedacht.

***Mein Trio-Buch* - eine Elementarschule des Ensemblespiels**
Alle Stimmen sind absichtlich so einfach wie möglich gehalten. Priorität haben also nicht satz- und kompositionstechnische Anforderungen, sondern leichte Spielbarkeit der dreistimmigen Sätze. Ist der Notentext erst einmal erlernt, kann mit der wirklichen Arbeit begonnen werden - der Verbesserung der Qualität des Ensemblespiels. Unterrichtsschwerpunkt soll die Feinabstimmung zwischen den einzelnen Stimmen sein in den Bereichen: Intonation, Rhythmus, Dynamik, Artikulation, Phrasierung, Bogeneinteilung, gemeinsames Atmen, gemeinsames Beginnen und Beenden einer Phrase u. a. Als Belohnung werden sich bei gründlicher Beschäftigung ein voller Ensembleklang und solide Zusammenspielfähigkeiten entwickeln, die nicht nur den Musizierenden Freude bereiten werden, sondern sicherlich auch den wohlwollenden Zuhörern.

Kerstin Wartberg

Reading Levels - Notenleseanforderungen

for the 2nd (=◆◆) and 3rd (=▣▣▣) violins — für die 2. (=◆◆) und die 3. Stimme (=▣▣▣)

Levels (beginner) Leseniveau (Anfänger)	very easy sehr leicht	easy leicht	medium mittel	difficult schwer
Reading challenges **Leseanforderungen**	open strings and a few fingered notes leere Saiten und wenig gegriffene Töne	small range, first finger pattern kleiner Tonumfang, erste Griffstellung	greater range, different finger patterns größerer Tonumfang, versch. Griffstellungen	chromatics, difficult finger patterns or rhythms Chromatik, schwere Griffe oder Rhythmen
Volume 1 - Heft 1	GRADE 1 1. STUFE	GRADE 2 2. STUFE	GRADE 3 3. STUFE	GRADE 4 4. STUFE
1. Twinkle, Twinkle - Leuchte, leuchte	▣▣▣		◆◆	
2. Lightly Row - Hänschen klein	▣▣▣		◆◆	
3. Song of the Wind - Fuchslied	▣▣▣		◆◆	
4. Go Tell Aunt Rhody - Tante Rhody	▣▣▣	◆◆		
5. O Come, Little Children - Ihr Kinderlein kommet	▣▣▣		◆◆	
6. May Song - Alle Vögel	▣▣▣		◆◆	
7. Long, Long Ago - Lang, lang ist's her	▣▣▣		◆◆	
8. Allegro	▣▣▣		◆◆	
9. Perpetual Motion	▣▣▣	◆◆		
10. Allegretto	▣▣▣		◆◆	
11. Andantino	▣▣▣		◆◆	
12. Etude - Etüde	▣▣▣		◆◆	
13. Minuet 1 - Menuett 1		▣▣▣	◆◆	
14. Minuet 2 - Menuett 2		▣▣▣		◆◆
15. Minuet 3 - Menuett 3		▣▣▣	◆◆	
16. The Happy Farmer - Der fröhliche Landmann		▣▣▣	◆◆	
17. Gavotte, *Gossec*		▣▣▣	◆◆	
Volume 2 - Heft 2	GRADE 1 1. STUFE	GRADE 2 2. STUFE	GRADE 3 3. STUFE	GRADE 4 4. STUFE
18. Chorus			▣▣▣	◆◆
19. Musette			▣▣▣+◆◆	
20. Hunters' Chorus - Jägerchor	▣▣▣		◆◆	
21. Long, Long Ago - Lang, lang ist's her	▣▣▣		◆◆	
22. Waltz - Walzer			▣▣▣	◆◆
23. Bourrée				▣▣▣+◆◆
24. The Two Grenadiers - Die zwei Grenadiere				▣▣▣+◆◆
25. Witche's Dance - Hexentanz			▣▣▣	◆◆
26. Gavotte from "Mignon"	▣▣▣			◆◆
27. Gavotte, *Lully*		▣▣▣	◆◆	
28. Minuet - Menuett, *Beethoven*		▣▣▣		◆◆
29. Minuet - Menuett, *Boccherini*		▣▣▣		◆◆

Dear Children:

You want to practice reading music!
I'm thrilled!

To help you I have written *My Trio Book*. At the end of this text you will find a chart in which all of the parts are rated according to difficulty. You should practice them in the order of the numbers in bold print.

How should you proceed?

1. Listen to the piece you are learning on the CD while you follow your part.

2. Listen to the piece again and clap the rhythm of your part.

3. Are there unfamiliar notes in your part? A chart on page 47 shows the names of all the notes and which fingers they should be played with. Now you can practice your part in a very slow tempo.

4. When you can play the part without mistakes, you may increase the tempo.

5. Now for the final test: Play along with the CD. Did it go smoothly? Bravo! Now check off the piece on the practice chart.

6. Repeat the pieces you have learned regularly and play them with the CD.

Now I hope you strive to become a good sight-reader. This will create new possibilities in discovering wonderful music!

Yours sincerely,
Kerstin Wartberg

Liebe Kinder:

Ihr wollt also Notenlesen üben!
Das freut mich sehr!

Um Euch dabei zu unterstützen, habe ich das *Trio-Buch* geschrieben. Nach diesem Text findet Ihr einen Übeplan, in dem alle Stimmen nach Schwierigkeitsgraden geordnet sind. Übt sie unbedingt in der Reihenfolge der fettgedruckten Nummern.

Wie sollt Ihr dabei vorgehen?

1. Hört Euch das zu erlernende Stück auf der CD an und schaut dabei in die Noten.

2. Hört Euch das Stück noch einmal an und klatscht den Rhythmus dazu.

3. Falls Ihr noch nicht alle Töne kennt, schaut auf den letzten Seiten des Heftes nach, wie die neuen Töne heißen und mit welchem Finger sie gespielt werden. Nun könnt Ihr die Stimme in sehr langsamem Tempo üben.

4. Wenn Ihr die Stimme fehlerlos gespielt habt, dürft Ihr das Tempo steigern.

5. Jetzt kommt der Abschlußtest: Spielt mit der CD zusammen. Ging es schon fließend? Bravo! Dann macht auf dem Übeplan ein Kreuzchen.

6. Wiederholt regelmäßig alle bisher erlernten Stücke und spielt sie mit CD-Begleitung.

Bei regelmäßigem Training werdet Ihr Euch sicherlich zu guten Blattspielern entwickeln und Euch dadurch eine Welt mit wunderschöner Musik eröffnen können!

Eure
Kerstin Wartberg

Practice Chart - Übeplan

Order Reihenfolge		GRADE 1: very easy 1. STUFE: sehr leicht		Vol., No. Heft, Nr.
❑	1	Twinkle, Twinkle - Leuchte, leuchte	3. Violin	1, 1
❑	2	Lightly Row - Hänschen klein	3. Violin	1, 2
❑	3	Song of the Wind - Fuchslied	3. Violin	1, 3
❑	4	Go Tell Aunt Rhody - Tante Rhody	3. Violin	1, 4
❑	5	O Come, Little Children - Ihr Kinderlein kommet	3. Violin	1, 5
❑	6	May Song - Alle Vögel	3. Violin	1, 6
❑	7	Long, Long Ago - Lang, lang ist's her	3. Violin	1, 7
❑	8	Allegro	3. Violin	1, 8
❑	9	Perpetual Motion	3. Violin	1, 9
❑	10	Allegretto	3. Violin	1, 10
❑	11	Andantino	3. Violin	1, 11
❑	12	Etude - Etüde	3. Violin	1, 12
❑	13	Hunters' Chorus - Jägerchor	3. Violin	2, 3
❑	14	Long, Long Ago - Lang, lang ist's her	3. Violin	2, 4
❑	15	Gavotte from "Mignon"	3. Violin	2, 9
		GRADE 2: easy 2. STUFE: leicht		**Vol., No. Heft, Nr.**
❑	16	Minuet 1 - Menuett 1	3. Violin	1, 13
❑	17	Minuet 2 - Menuett 2	3. Violin	1, 14
❑	18	Minuet 3 - Menuett 3	3. Violin	1, 15
❑	19	The Happy Farmer - Der fröhliche Landmann	3. Violin	1, 16
❑	20	Gavotte, *Gossec*	3. Violin	1, 17
❑	21	Gavotte, *Lully*	3. Violin	2, 10
❑	22	Minuet, *Beethoven*	3. Violin	2, 11
❑	23	Minuet, *Boccherini*	3. Violin	2, 12
❑	24	Go Tell Aunt Rhody – Tante Rhody	2. Violin	1, 4
❑	25	Perpetual Motion	2. Violin	1, 9

		GRADE 3: medium 3. STUFE: mittel		Vol., No. Heft, Nr.
❑	26	Twinkle, Twinkle - Leuchte, leuchte	2. Violin	1, 1
❑	27	Lightly Row - Hänschen klein	2. Violin	1, 2
❑	28	Song of the Wind - Fuchslied	2. Violin	1, 3
❑	29	Come, Little Children - Ihr Kinderlein kommet	2. Violin	1, 5
❑	30	May Song - Alle Vögel	2. Violin	1, 6
❑	31	Long, Long Ago - Lang, lang ist's her	2. Violin	1, 7
❑	32	Allegro	2. Violin	1, 8
❑	33	Allegretto	2. Violin	1, 10
❑	34	Andantino	2. Violin	1, 11
❑	35	Etude - Etüde	2. Violin	1, 12
❑	36	Minuet 1 - Menuett 1	2. Violin	1, 13
❑	37	Minuet 3 - Menuett 3	2. Violin	1, 15
❑	38	The Happy Farmer - Der fröhliche Landmann	2. Violin	1, 16
❑	39	Gavotte, *Gossec*	2. Violin	1, 17
❑	40	Musette, *Bach*	2. Violin	2, 2
❑	41	Hunters' Chorus - Jägerchor	2. Violin	2, 3
❑	42	Long, Long Ago - Lang, lang ist's her	2. Violin	2, 4
❑	43	Gavotte, *Lully*	2. Violin	2, 10
❑	44	Chorus, *Händel*	3. Violin	2, 1
❑	45	Musette, *Bach*	3. Violin	2, 2
❑	46	Waltz - Walzer	3. Violin	2, 5
❑	47	Witches' Dance - Hexentanz	3. Violin	2, 8
		GRADE 4: difficult 4. STUFE: schwer		**Vol., No. Heft, Nr.**
❑	48	Minuet 2 - Menuett 2	2. Violin	1, 14
❑	49	Chorus, *Händel*	2. Violin	2, 1
❑	50	Waltz - Walzer	2. Violin	2, 5
❑	51	Bourrée, *Händel*	3. Violin	2, 6
❑	52	Bourrée, *Händel*	2. Violin	2, 6
❑	53	The Two Grenadiers - Die zwei Grenadiere	3. Violin	2, 7
❑	54	The Two Grenadiers - Die zwei Grenadiere	2. Violin	2, 7
❑	55	Witches' Dance - Hexentanz	2. Violin	2, 8
❑	56	Gavotte from "Mignon"	2. Violin	2, 9
❑	57	Minuet, *Beethoven*	2. Violin	2, 11
❑	58	Minuet, *Boccherini*	2. Violin	2, 12

1. Twinkle, Twinkle, Little Star - Leuchte, leuchte kleiner Stern

Folk Song
Volkslied

Var. A

Theme - Thema

2. Lightly Row - Hänschen klein

Folk Song
Volkslied

3. Song of the Wind - Fuchslied

Folk Song
Volkslied

4. Go Tell Aunt Rhody - Tante Rhody

Folk Song
Volkslied

5. O Come, Little Children - Ihr Kinderlein kommet

Folk Song
Volkslied

6. May Song - Alle Vögel sind schon da

Folk Song
Volkslied

7. Long, Long Ago - Lang, lang ist's her

T. H. Bayly

8. Allegro

S. Suzuki

9. Perpetual Motion

S. Suzuki

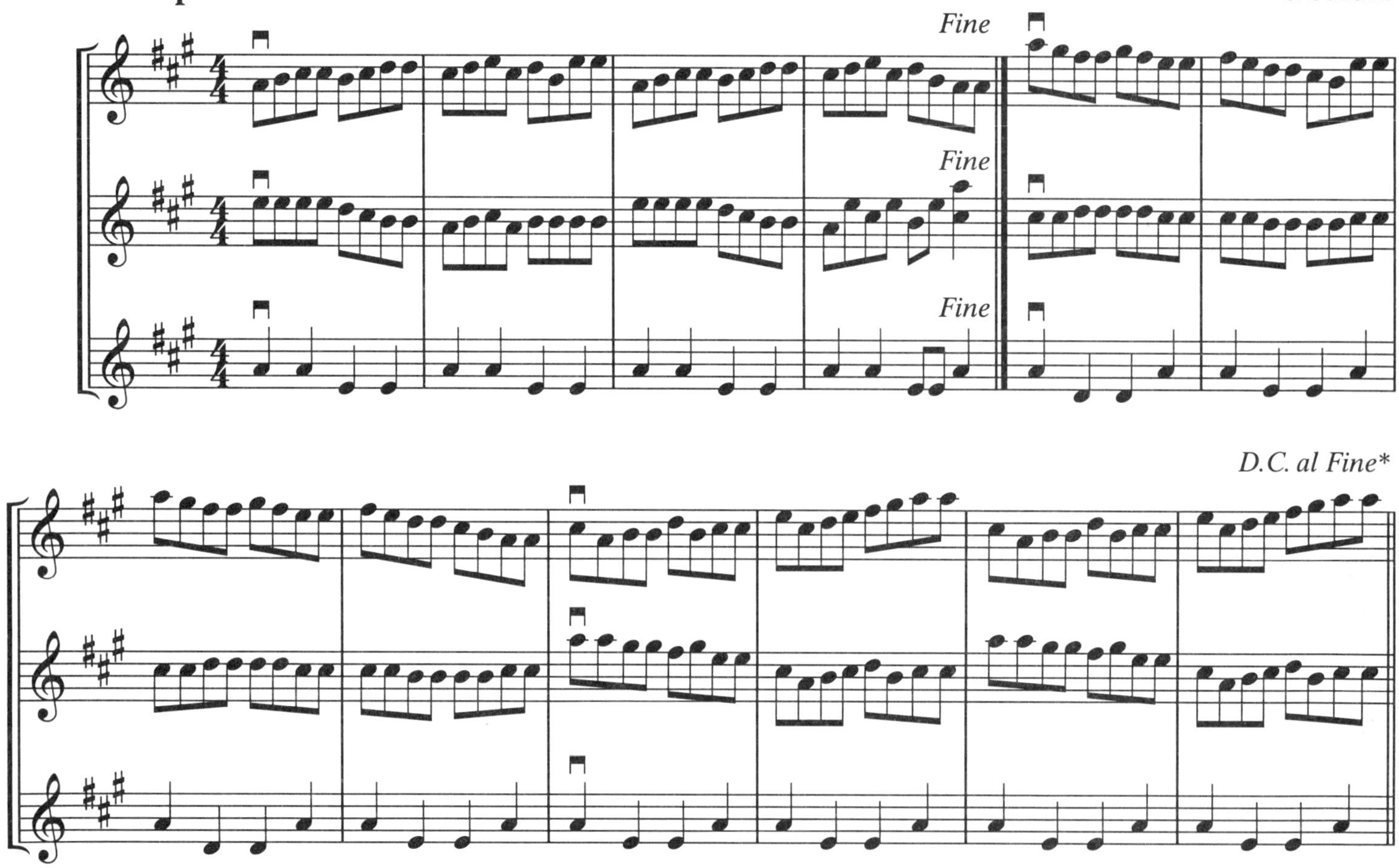

* Go back to the beginning and keep playing until you reach the word *Fine* (*Fine* = Finish).
Beginne noch einmal von vorne und spiele bis zu dem Wort *Fine* (*Fine* = Schluß).

10. Allegretto

S. Suzuki

11. Andantino

S. Suzuki

12. Etude - Etüde

S. Suzuki

13. Minuet 1 - Menuett 1

J. S. Bach

1.ending-Endung
2. ending-Endung
p
p
p
mf
mf
mf

14. Minuet 2 - Menuett 2

J. S. Bach

15. Minuet 3 - Menuett 3

J. S. Bach

f
mf
mf
p
p
f
f
f

16. The Happy Farmer - Der fröhliche Landmann

R. Schumann

17. Gavotte

F. J. Gossec

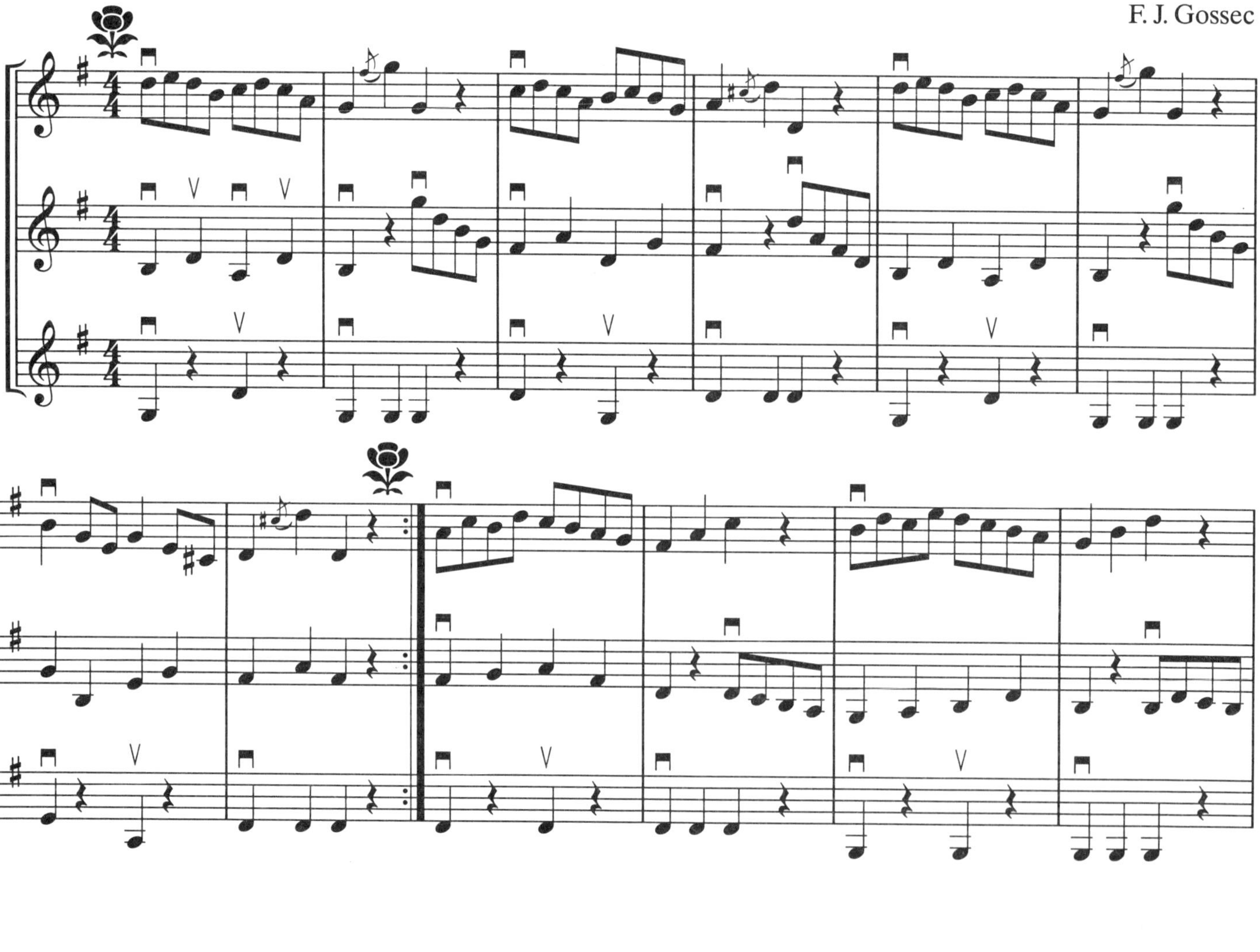

* Go back again to the beginning and keep playing until you reach the word *Fine* - but now without repeating the first part!
Beginne noch einmal von vorne und spiele bis zu dem Wort *Fine* - nun aber ohne die Wiederholung des ersten Teils!

18. Chorus from "Judas Maccabaeus"

G. F. Händel

19. Musette

J. S. Bach

20. Hunters' Chorus - Jägerchor

C. M. von Weber

ff
1.
2.
f

21. Long, Long Ago - Lang, lang ist's her

T. H. Bayly

Variation

22. Waltz - Walzer

J. Brahms

23. Bourrée

G. F. Händel

24. The Two Grenadiers - Die zwei Grenadiere

R. Schumann

f a tempo
f a tempo
f a tempo
p
mf
p
p
mf
mf
f
f
f

25. Theme from "Witches Dance" - Thema aus "Hexentanz"

N. Paganini

meno mosso
p
p
p
rit.
rit.
rit.
f a tempo
mf a tempo
mf a tempo

26. Gavotte from "Mignon" - Gavotte aus "Mignon"

A. Thomas

rit.
mf a tempo
rit.
p a tempo
rit.
p a tempo

rit.
a tempo
mf
pizz.
p
rit.
a tempo
pizz.
rit.
a tempo
p

1.
2.
mf
arco
mf
arco
mf
pizz.
p
pizz.
p
pizz.
p

27. Gavotte

J. B. Lully

rit.
rit.
rit.
rit.
rit.
rit.

28. Minuet - Menuett

L. van Beethoven

Trio
mf
mf
mf
1. Violin
1. Geige
p
p
rit.
rit.
rit.
1.
2.
D.C. al Fine
f a tempo
f a tempo
f a tempo

29. Minuet - Menuett

L. Boccherini

Fine
Trio

D.C. al Fine

Table of finger patterns for the first position
Grifftabelle für die 1. Lage

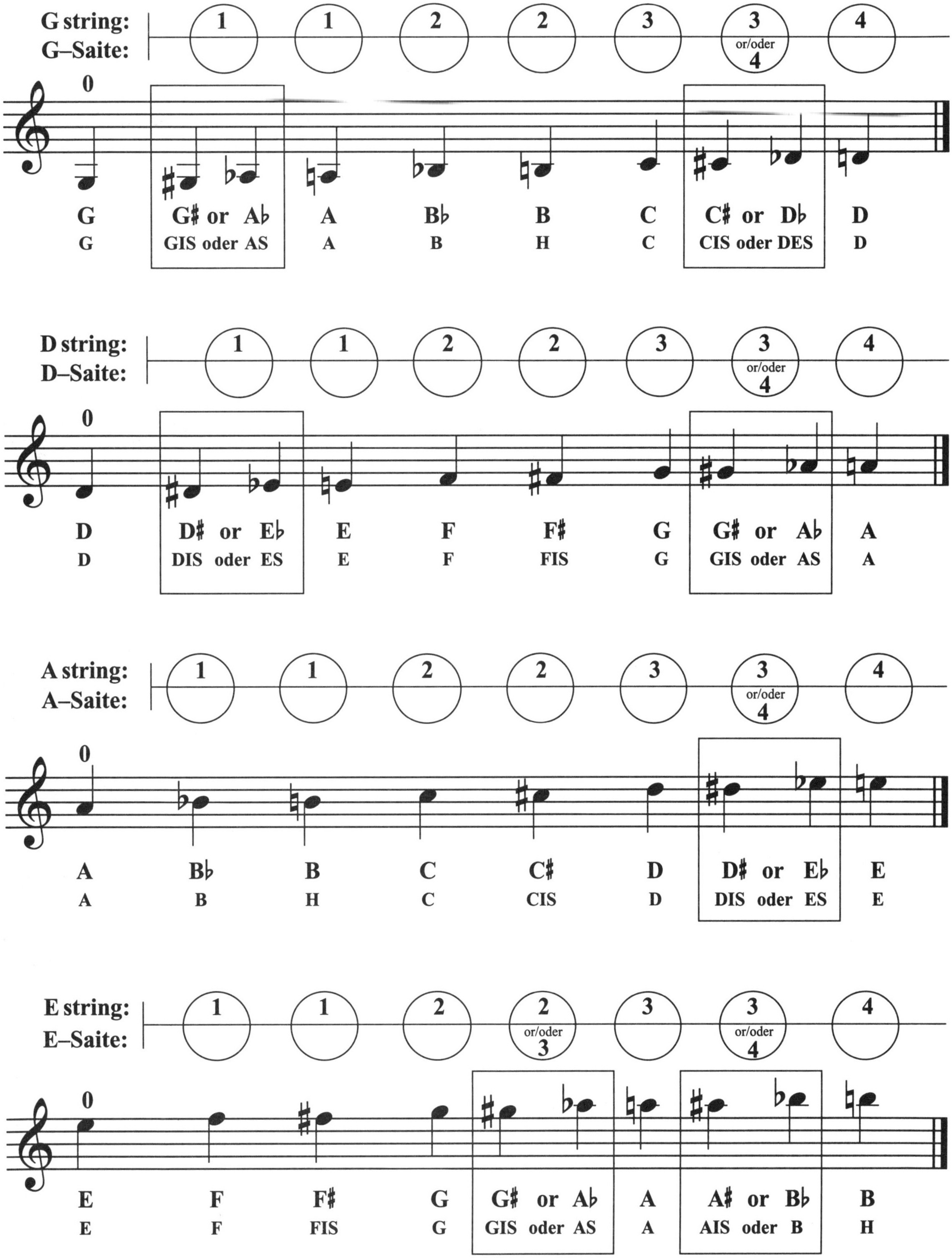